Buddhist VIHARA

Anita Ganeri

Contents

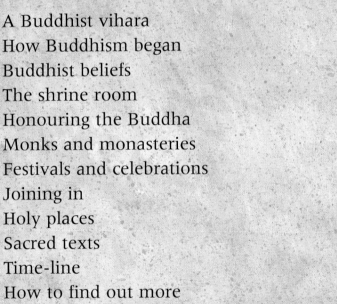

A & C BLACK • LONDON

A Buddhist vihara

This book is about a Buddhist *vihara*, a holy place where Buddhists worship and where Buddhist monks live. The children featured in this book visited the London Buddhist Vihara in Chiswick, West London. They wanted to find out more about Buddhism, the way of life which Buddhists follow.

▲ *The children and their teacher were welcomed by the abbot, the Venerable Dr Medagama Vajiragnana who is the Head of the* **vihara**. *They brought some baskets of fruit and flowers to offer before the statue of the Buddha.*

The word *vihara* means a Buddhist temple or monastery. The first *viharas* were simple huts, built by early followers of the Buddha, in northern India, where Buddhism began. The monks stayed in these huts during the rainy season, when the weather made it difficult for them to travel around India teaching the message of the Buddha. Today, there are many beautiful *viharas* and temples - both old and new - all over the world.

*◁ As they entered the **vihara**, the children looked at a painting of the Buddha, the founder of Buddhism. The picture was painted by a Sri Lankan artist, Lal Ratnayake, who lives in London.*

The present London Buddhist Vihara was opened on 21 May 1994. It is one of several important centres for *Theravada* Buddhism in Britain. You can find out more about *Theravada* Buddhism throughout this book. The first London Buddhist Vihara was founded in 1926 by Anagarika Dharmapala, a Sri Lankan. The *vihara* has moved home several times since then. Everyone is very happy with its new, more spacious building. The children learned that it used to be a social club, and the shrine room was once a billiards' room! It is now dedicated to the Buddha.

The colours of the Buddhist flag symbolise different qualities: blue is for confidence, yellow is for holiness, red is for wisdom, white is for purity and orange is for freedom from desire. The sixth stripe is a mixture of these five colours. ▼

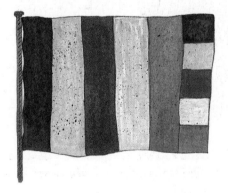

*▲ On special days, the brightly-coloured Buddhist flag is raised outside the **vihara**. This happens every year on Buddha Day (see page 18). Here the ceremony is being watched by the abbot and a group of **devotees**. A similar ceremony was held on the day the **vihara** was opened.*

Apart from the shrine room, the *vihara* has a meeting hall, a teaching and meditation hall, a library, offices, a bookstall and a kitchen. There are also living quarters for the monks. Many of the people who come to the *vihara* are Buddhists from Sri Lanka. The *vihara* is not simply a place for worship but also a place where they can meet their friends and celebrate their Sri Lankan culture. But Buddhists of many other nationalities also visit the *vihara* to take part in religious ceremonies and celebrate festivals.

How Buddhism began

Buddhism began about 2,500 years ago in northern India. Its founder was a king's son, called Siddhartha Gautama. When he was born, a wise man foretold his future. He said that Siddhartha would become a great holy man, a Buddha. But wishing his son to be a great king, his father kept him inside the royal palace, surrounded by luxury and sheltered from the outside world.

At the age of 29, Prince Siddhartha secretly left the palace, accompanied by a faithful attendant. What he saw changed his life. For the first time he saw a weak old man, a very sick man and a dead man. He had never seen ageing, suffering and death before. Then he saw a holy man who, despite having nothing, seemed happy and contented. Siddhartha decided to follow the holy man's example and find an answer to the problem of suffering. That night, he left the palace for good and began his search for the truth.

▲ *Look at this painting. Can you see the 'Four Sights' – the old man, the sick man, the dead man and the holy man?*

For six long years, Siddhartha lived in the forest with five holy companions. His life was very hard. He ate and drank little, and slept under trees or in caves. But he did not find the answer.

Then, one day, in the small village of Bodh Gaya, he sat down under a tree to *meditate*. There he gained *enlightenment*. He saw why people suffered and how their suffering could be stopped. From that time on, he became known as the Buddha, a title which means 'the *enlightened* one'.

*In the **vihara**, the children looked at a silver image ▶ of the Buddha sitting **meditating** underneath a tree. This tree is known as a **Bodhi tree**. The word **Bodhi** means 'wisdom' or 'enlightenment'. It is the name given to the type of tree underneath which the Buddha gained **enlightenment**.*

◀ *In the shrine room, the abbot told the children that he had brought the **Bodhi tree** sapling with him from Sri Lanka. A cutting from the original **Bodhi tree** at Bodh Gaya, under which the Buddha gained **enlightenment**, was planted at the sacred site of Anuradhapura in Sri Lanka about 2,200 years ago. This ancient tree is still growing.*

The Buddha spent the rest of his life travelling around India and teaching his message. He and his followers lived as monks. He passed away, at the age of 80, in the town of Kushinagara. Legend says that when he died, a great earthquake shook the earth.

Buddhist beliefs

After the Buddha's *enlightenment*, he travelled to Sarnath and gave his first sermon in the Deer Park. It was called 'the Sermon of the Turning of the Wheel of Law'. The Buddha explained that life was like a wheel, turning and turning in an endless circle of being born, growing old, dying and being reborn. The only way to stop the wheel turning was to gain *enlightenment* and reach *nirvana*, a state of perfect peace and happiness. To do this, people needed to follow the Buddha's teachings.

◀ *A Buddhist temple in the Deer Park at Sarnath.*

*The children looked at a **dharma**-wheel. **Dharma** means the Buddha's teaching. Each of the eight spokes of the wheel stands for one of the eight steps on the 'Middle Way'.* ▼

The Four Noble Truths form the first part of the Buddha's teachings.

1. Human life is full of *dukkha*. This is a *Sanskrit* word which means 'that which is difficult to endure', which could describe physical pain, for example, or feeling unhappy.
2. The reason for *dukkha* is people's selfishness and greed. People are never content with what they have. They always want more.
3. There is a way to end *dukkha*.
4. The way to end *dukkha* is to live your life according to the 'Middle Way', which is known as the 'Noble Eightfold Path'.

The children asked about the flowers on the doors of the shrine room. They discovered that these were lotus flowers, a very important Buddhist symbol. The lotus flowers stand for goodness and purity. They also show how people must rise above the trials of life to reach **enlightenment**, just as the lotus flowers rise above water to bloom.

The Buddha taught people to follow the 'Middle Way', between the extremes of hardship and luxury. Then they could lead better, more caring lives, on their way to gaining *enlightenment*. The path has eight steps:

A woman brings an offering of food to a Buddhist shrine in Sri Lanka. Generosity is considered to be a very important part of Buddhist practice. Buddhists believe that if you lead a good life, you will be reborn in happy circumstances. A bad life leads you to a miserable state. This is called **karma** and **vipaka**; the law of cause and effect.

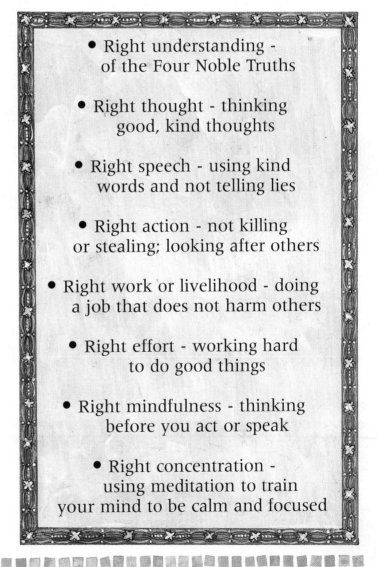

- Right understanding - of the Four Noble Truths

- Right thought - thinking good, kind thoughts

- Right speech - using kind words and not telling lies

- Right action - not killing or stealing; looking after others

- Right work or livelihood - doing a job that does not harm others

- Right effort - working hard to do good things

- Right mindfulness - thinking before you act or speak

- Right concentration - using meditation to train your mind to be calm and focused

Buddhists try to follow the Buddha's teachings in everything they do. They follow the 'Three Jewels of Buddhism' as their guides through life. These are the Buddha, the *Dharma* (his teaching) and the *Sangha* (the noble community of monks and nuns). They are called 'jewels' or 'gems' because they are so precious.

This is a Buddhist temple in Tibet. The monks follow a form of Mahayana Buddhism which came to Tibet from India and China about 1300 years ago.

Although Buddhists commit themselves to following the Buddha, they do not worship him as a god but honour him as one who gained *enlightenment* and became a supreme teacher. The Buddha did not want people to follow him blindly but to be responsible for their own actions.

For Buddhists, showing compassion and care towards other people and sharing things with others are very important. In their everyday lives, they also follow a set of guidelines, called the 'Five *Precepts*', or 'Undertakings'. These are:

- *Not killing or harming living things.*
- *Not stealing or taking things unless they are freely given.*
- *Not committing adultery.*
- *Not speaking unkindly, carelessly or untruthfully.*
- *Not drinking alcohol or taking intoxicating drugs.*

All Buddhists follow the teachings of the Buddha. But they have different ways of understanding these teachings. The two main groups, or schools, of Buddhism are *Theravada* and *Mahayana*. The London Buddhist Vihara is a centre for *Theravada* Buddhism. *Theravada* Buddhists follow Siddhartha Gautama, the historical Buddha, as their guide. *Mahayana* Buddhists believe in many different Buddhas and god-like figures, called *bodhisattvas*. Both schools agree on all the Buddha's teachings, but there are differences in the way they practise Buddhism which vary from country to country.

◀ *The Dalai Lama is the spiritual leader of Tibet. Since the Chinese invasion of Tibet in the 1960s, the Dalai Lama has established his government in exile in Dharamsala, India. He is widely known and deeply respected. He travels around the world, talking to people about Tibet, Buddhism and peace. When the Dalai Lama visited London in 1988, he met the abbot of the London Buddhist Vihara.*

Another type of Mahayana Buddhism ▶ *is followed in Japan. It is called Zen, which is a form of **meditation**. Many Zen monasteries have a sand garden, like this one. Its simple, natural design helps the monks to focus their minds for **meditation**.*

The shrine room

When Buddhists visit the *vihara*, one of the first things they do is to take off their shoes, as a mark of respect. Then they go quietly into the shrine room to kneel down in front of a large, golden image of the Buddha to pay respect. This is called *puja*. You can read about *puja* on pages 12-15.

*In the shrine room, the children were shown the golden image of the Buddha. They saw the **Bodhi tree** sapling on the left of the Buddha and the silver **stupa** on the right. Two smaller brass **stupas** stood on either side. In front of the shrine, **devotees** had placed offerings of fruit, flowers, candles and incense.*

*In early types of Buddhist art, the Buddha was not shown in person but by symbols. These included a **stupa** (like this one), a wheel, a footprint, a lotus flower, a **Bodhi tree** and a royal umbrella held over an empty throne.*

In some religions, temples and other holy places are seen as God's home on earth. But this is not the same in Buddhism. When Buddhists visit the *vihara*, they do not go to worship a god but to show honour and respect to the Buddha as a great teacher and to renew their commitment to the 'Three Jewels'. They trust that this will help bring them peace and happiness in this and in any future lives.

The image of the Buddha in the shrine room reminds people of the Buddha's teaching and of his special qualities of compassion, peacefulness and kindness. It also reminds them that, by following his example, they too can gain *enlightenment*.

◀ *The children discovered that every part of the Buddha's image tells a story. His tightly-curled hair shows that he was a very holy man. The positions of his hands and fingers also have a special meaning. Here, they show* **meditation** *and concentration.*

Many Buddhists have a small shrine at home where they can pay their respects every day. ▼

Buddhists do not have to go to the *vihara* at a special time or day of the week. Many people try to go on Full Moon days, which are considered to be holy days. People also visit the *vihara* to *meditate* with other Buddhists and to attend talks and classes. You can read more about *meditation* on page 14.

Honouring the Buddha

On weekdays and Saturdays, the monks perform *puja* three times a day, in the morning, at midday and in the evening. On Sundays, a special *puja* for children is held at 3 p.m., with a *puja* for adults at 5 p.m. *Devotees* can take part in any of these services, although the Sunday service is the most popular.

▲ *The children listened to the gong which is struck at the beginning of the puja. At the same time, the monks and worshippers chant the words 'Sadhu, Sadhu, Sadhu' to signal that the devotions are about to start.*

When people arrive at the *vihara* for *puja*, they take off their shoes and enter the shrine room. Then they sit or kneel in front of the image of the Buddha, with their heads bowed and hands together.

The first part of the *puja* is the *Vandana*, or 'Homage' to the Buddha. The *devotees* recite the words, 'Honour to the Blessed One, the Exalted One, the Fully-Enlightened One!' three times. Then they repeat their commitment to the 'Three Jewels' by saying this verse three times after the monks:

'I go to the Buddha as my Refuge
I go to the Dharma as my Refuge
I go to the Sangha as my Refuge.'

Next, the *devotees* repeat the 'Five *Precepts'* after the monks.

▲ *The children had brought baskets of offerings with them. They placed these on the shrine in front of the Buddha.*

The words of the *puja* are given in this book in English. But in the *vihara* they are recited in an ancient Indian language, called *Pali*. You can read more about *Pali* on pages 26 and 27.

Devotees can bring offerings of flowers, candles and incense to place on the shrine in front of the Buddha at any time as a sign of respect or devotion.

Each of the offerings has a special meaning. Flowers look fresh and colourful but they eventually wilt and die. This is a reminder of the Buddha's teaching that everything changes. Nothing lasts for ever. And just as a candle lights up a dark room, so the light of the Buddha's teaching helps make the darkness of ignorance disappear. The sweet smell of incense is a reminder of the beauty and sweetness of the Buddha's teachings.

▲

This boy is placing lotus flowers in front of an image of the Buddha in a temple in Sri Lanka.

◄

Brightly-coloured prayer flags are given as offerings to decorate a temple in the sacred city of Anuradhapura in Sri Lanka.

When the offerings have been made, three more verses are chanted in praise of the 'Three Jewels' - the Buddha, the *Dharma* and the *Sangha*. These are followed by the *Metta Sutta*, a Buddhist sermon, or talk, on the importance of *metta* which means 'loving kindness'. Here are the words of the main part of the *Metta Sutta*:

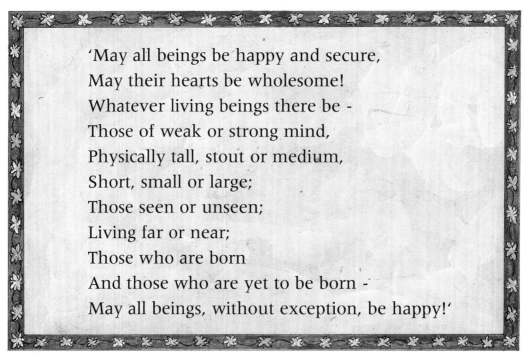

'May all beings be happy and secure,
May their hearts be wholesome!
Whatever living beings there be -
Those of weak or strong mind,
Physically tall, stout or medium,
Short, small or large;
Those seen or unseen;
Living far or near;
Those who are born
And those who are yet to be born -
May all beings, without exception, be happy!'

The *puja* ends with *meditation* on the theme of loving kindness, and with verses of thanksgiving and blessings. *Meditation* is a very important part of Buddhist practice. Buddhists believe that training their minds and concentrating on positive thoughts and feelings will bring them closer to *enlightenment*. Buddhists *meditate* on their own and in groups. The *vihara* runs its own weekly classes where people can learn how to *meditate*.

The children asked how people learned to meditate. The abbot told them that he sits cross-legged on the floor, with his eyes closed, breathing calmly and evenly. Then he tries to concentrate his mind specifically on breathing. People find that meditation takes a lot of practice. It isn't easy to stop other thoughts getting in the way!

After the *puja*, the monks chant verses from the sacred books. These verses are called *pirith*. They are thought to protect people from harm. They may be chanted when people are ill or worried about something, or to mark important events such as the birth of a baby, a marriage or the move to a new home. Some very special *pirith* ceremonies continue for a full week, day and night, without a break in the chanting, the monks taking part in relays.

▲ *The sacred thread which is held during the* **pirith** *ceremony is made up of three strands which represent the 'Three Jewels', the Buddha, the* **Dharma** *and the* **Sangha**.

During the *pirith* ceremony, the congregation is bound together by a single thread. One end of this thread is placed in a pot of water. The water is made holy by the chanting of the sacred verses during the ceremony. Afterwards the water is poured into the cupped hands of the *devotees* for them to drink. The holy thread is cut into pieces and divided amongst the *devotees* to be worn around the wrist or neck. The purpose is to maintain an unbroken link between them and the 'Three Jewels'.

Monks and monasteries

Three monks, or *bhikkhus*, live in the London Buddhist Vihara, together with the abbot. The first Buddhist monks were five holy men who had lived in the forest with the Buddha before his *enlightenment*.

Later, the Buddha *ordained* his son, Rahula, and his cousin, Ananda. Rahula was the child of Prince Siddhartha's marriage to Princess Yasodhara, before he left the palace and adopted a new way of life.

After the Buddha's *enlightenment*, he lived as a monk, travelling around India and inspiring others to follow the holy life.

Buddhist monks live simple lives, dedicated to studying, practising and teaching the Buddha's message. They obey a set of 227 monastic rules, called the *vinaya*.

▲ *The Venerable Dr Medagama Vajiragnana became Head of the **vihara** in 1985. In 1990, he was appointed by the Supreme Sangha Council of Sri Lanka as Sangha Nayake of Great Britain. This means that Ven. Dr Vajiragnana is the leader of the Sri Lankan Buddhist community in this country.*

The children asked the monks why they wear saffron-coloured robes and why they shave their heads. The monks told them ▷ *that saffron robes date back to the time of the first Buddhist monks. Most of them lived in forests, and found that the saffron colour harmonised very well with their natural surroundings and did not upset the other animals living there. They shave their heads to show that they are not vain and as a sign that they are not concerned with the material world.*

Traditionally, the monks are only allowed to own eight items. These are called the 'Eight Requisites'. They include three robes, an *alms* bowl, a belt, a razor, a water-strainer and a sewing needle. Everything the monks need is donated by *devotees* and well wishers, including their food. This is just as it was in the Buddha's day.

◀ *These young boys in Tibet are learning to become monks.*

*People offering food and lotus blossoms to monks in Thailand. The monks take the food back to the **vihara** and share it out amongst themselves.* ▼

The monks of the London Buddhist Vihara lead the *puja* services, greet visitors, including visiting monks, and look after the daily running of the *vihara*.

They also give talks about the *Dharma*, and run *meditation* classes and courses in *Pali* and *Sinhala* (a language of Sri Lanka).

The monks visit schools and universities and give talks to both Buddhist and non-Buddhist societies. They visit hospitals, attend funerals and perform other religious ceremonies, such as marriages and house-warming blessings.

Festivals and celebrations

There are many Buddhist festivals throughout the year. The most important remember events in the Buddha's life. Some are celebrated by Buddhists all over the world. Others are special to a particular country. The *vihara* is busy on festival days with visitors arriving to take part in the *puja* and to bring offerings for the monks.

Full Moon Days

Poya days, or Full Moon days, are particularly holy for Buddhists. They happen once a month. The most important events in the Buddha's life are believed to have happened on them. On these days, Buddhists visit the *vihara*, dressed in simple, white clothes. They also observe 'Eight *Precepts'* for the day. These are the Five *Precepts*, plus three others - not eating after midday, not singing, dancing or wearing perfume, and not using luxurious beds or chairs.

Vesak - Buddha Day

The most important festival of the year is celebrated on the Full Moon day of May. This is called *Vesak*, or Buddha Day. It marks the Buddha's birth, his *enlightenment* and his passing away.

People visit the *vihara* and decorate their homes with lamps and flowers and send *Vesak* cards to their friends.

*On **Vesak**, or Buddha Day, the **devotees**, dressed in white for the day, eat a meal prepared and offered by helpers at the **vihara**. Many Buddhists are vegetarians because they do not believe in killing animals.*

◀ *This amazing **Vesak** decoration in Sri Lanka shows the Buddha leaving his father's palace in his chariot. It is surrounded by other scenes from the Buddha's life.*

In the London Buddhist Vihara, there is a special programme of *meditation* and talks. The day begins with the hoisting of the Buddhist flag outside the *vihara*. Children enjoy a similar but shorter programme of songs and stories.

Children's Day

In March or April, when Christians are celebrating Easter, Children's Day is held in the *vihara*. This is called *Rahula Dhamma (Dharma)* Day. Rahula was the Buddha's son and one of his followers.

The children give a concert which includes singing and dancing. Then they listen to *Jataka* stories. These tell of the Buddha's past lives in which he was born as an animal, such as a hare, elephant or lion. The stories teach the value of sharing, kindness, patience and other good qualities. Afterwards there is a party and every child leaves with a present.

*A painting of a **Jataka** story.* ▼

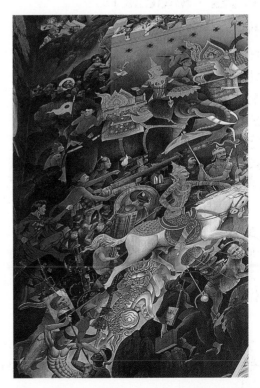

Poson

The festival of *Poson* is celebrated on the Full Moon day of June. This is a special day in Sri Lanka. It marks the day on which Emperor Ashoka's son, Mahinda, officially brought Buddhism to the island in the 3rd century BCE. The Buddhist flag is hoisted at the *vihara* and there is a day-long programme of *meditation*, talks and *chanting*. *Devotees* practise generosity by making offerings and donations of money to the *vihara*.

The festival of Esala is celebrated in Kandy, Sri Lanka with a procession through the streets.

Many Buddhist pilgrims travel to India to visit the Deer Park at Sarnath and other holy places in the Buddha's life. ▼

Esala - Dhamma Day

Held on the Full Moon day of July, the festival of *Esala* celebrates several events in Buddhist history, including the preaching of the Buddha's first sermon in the Deer Park at Sarnath.

It is also the day on which the first Sri Lankan monk was *ordained* in the 3rd century BCE. He was Prince Arittha, the nephew of the king. The day is celebrated at the *vihara* with *meditation*, sermons and *chanting* and *devotees* bringing offerings.

The Festival of the Tooth Relic

On the August Full Moon, a special procession takes place in Kandy, Sri Lanka when over a hundred elephants parade through the city. One elephant carries a copy of a casket on its back. The original casket is kept safely in a nearby temple. It contains a very precious *relic* - a sacred tooth, which belonged to the Buddha himself.

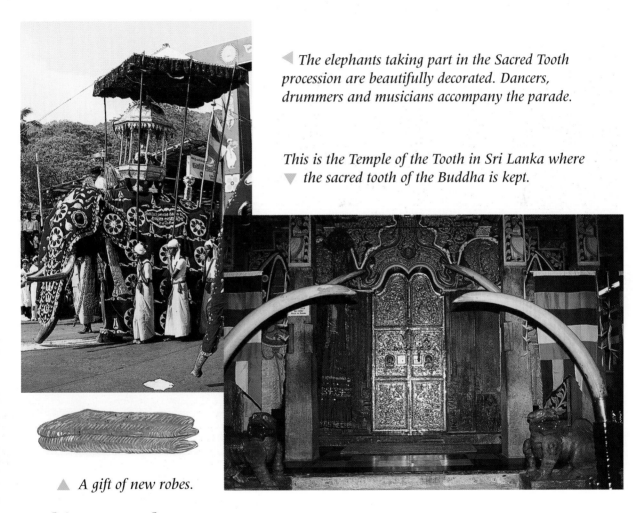

◀ *The elephants taking part in the Sacred Tooth procession are beautifully decorated. Dancers, drummers and musicians accompany the parade.*

This is the Temple of the Tooth in Sri Lanka where ▼ *the sacred tooth of the Buddha is kept.*

▲ *A gift of new robes.*

Kathina - Sangha Day

The festival of *Kathina* takes place in November, at the end of the rainy season retreat in Sri Lanka and other Asian countries. During the rains, the monks traditionally stayed in a *vihara* because they could not travel. To mark *Kathina*, *devotees* visit the *vihara* with gifts for the monks to thank them for all their work. The most important of these are new robes.

Joining in

Some people are born into Buddhist families. Others join Buddhism from another faith, or become Buddhists later in life. They do this during a short ceremony when they repeat their commitment to the 'Three Jewels' and to the 'Five *Precepts*', using the same words that form part of the *puja* (see page 12).

▲ *The* **vihara** *is a popular meeting place for members of different faiths. In May or June each year, the monks at the* **vihara** *take part in an interfaith* **pilgrimage** *across London to visit different places of worship.*

In a Buddhist family, parents try to bring their children up according to the Buddha's teachings. When a baby is born, its parents take it to the *vihara* to be blessed. The Buddha taught that it is very important for children to obey their parents and look after them in their old age. Parents should care for their children and teach them to be kind, generous and hardworking.

At the London Buddhist Vihara, there are many opportunities for children to join in. Each Sunday, before the main *puja*, there is a *Dhamma (Dharma)* School for children, where they can learn more about the Buddha and his teachings. The children are taught Buddhist sayings and are encouraged to draw pictures of the Buddha. They can also learn the Sri Lankan language, *Sinhala*. Other children who are not Buddhists come to the *vihara* too. Each week, local children hold their school assembly in the meeting hall.

▲ *In the sermon hall, the children looked at a huge, stone image of the Buddha. There is also a special chair for the abbot to sit in when he gives his sermons and talks.*

*The children looked at some of the books in the **vihara** library. The library contains about 3,500 books, in **Pali**, English, **Sinhala** and other languages. It also has many pamphlets and periodicals covering all aspects of Buddhism.*

▶

The monks run classes and courses for adults in Buddhism, *meditation*, *Pali* and *Sinhala*. There are classes almost every day of the week. There is also a library and bookstall for visitors to use.

The *vihara* publishes its own journal, called *Samadhi*, or 'calm meditation'. It has articles and features on Buddhism, together with information about the classes and about other activities which are held at the *vihara*.

Holy places

Some of the holiest places for Buddhists to visit were mentioned by the Buddha in his teachings and are linked to events in the Buddha's life. These include the Buddha's birthplace in Lumbini, Nepal; Bodh Gaya where he gained *enlightenment*; Sarnath where he gave his first sermon, and Kushinagara where he passed away. The last three places are all in India. Buddhists from all over the world visit these places to honour the Buddha. They hope that these journeys, or *pilgrimages*, will help them earn merit and inspire them to follow a spiritual life.

One of the holiest places in Sri Lanka is a mountain called Sri Pada. Pilgrims climb a long flight of steps to the top. At the summit is a stone with a mark like a footprint on it, believed to have been made by the Buddha himself.

Pilgrims also travel to the ancient city of Anuradhapura where they visit the sacred *Bodhi tree*, said to have grown from a cutting of the original *Bodhi tree* in Bodh Gaya.

◀ *Every year, thousands of pilgrims visit the Mahabodhi Temple in Bodh Gaya. The Temple was built on the spot where the Buddha gained enlightenment.*

*The sacred **Bodhi tree** at Anuradhapura and the monk who looks after it.* ▶

The earliest Buddhist shrines were dome-shaped monuments, called *stupas*. The first eight *stupas* were built after the Buddha's death, in places important to him. His body was *cremated* and his ashes divided up and placed inside them. Today, there are *stupas* all over the Buddhist world. Some hold the ashes of important monks, or copies of the sacred texts. Some are sacred symbols. When Buddhists visit a *stupa*, they walk around it three times, keeping it on their right-hand side. This reminds them of the 'Three Jewels'.

▶ *This is one of the most ancient **stupas** in India. It was built in Sanchi by the Emperor Ashoka who converted to Buddhism after a bloody battle. Each of the four gateways is beautifully carved with scenes from the Jataka stories.*

◀

*This is the Shwe Dagon Pagoda in Myanmar, (Burma). A pagoda is a type of **stupa**. This pagoda is said to hold eight of the Buddha's hairs. It is very sacred indeed. The dome is covered in gleaming gold, donated by **devotees**.*

Sacred texts

The sacred texts of the *Theravada* Buddhists are a collection of writings called the *Pali Canon*. They are also known as the *Tripitaka* which means 'Three Baskets', or collections. The first contains rules for monks to follow. The second has the Buddha's teachings and stories about his life. The third contains more teachings.

The 'Pali Canon' may have been called the 'Three Baskets' because it was first written on palm leaves which were stored in baskets. ▶

◀ *The children looked at the ancient, palm-leaf books which are kept in the **vihara**.*

The sacred books were written on palm leaves, shaped into rectangular pages. They were not written in pen but inscribed with a stylus (a thin, metal stick) on both sides of the page. The writers had to be careful not to press too hard. The wooden covers of the books were carved or painted.

The books were made by monks using a technique which is hundreds of years old. The monks spent their whole lives copying out texts. In some monasteries in Sri Lanka, books are still made like this today.

Theravada Buddhists use the teachings of the *Pali Canon* to guide them through their lives. Monks chant, study and explain the texts to the *devotees*. They learn large parts by heart.

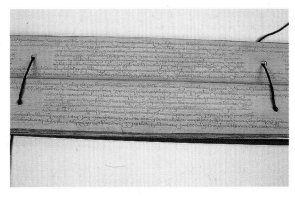

Passages from the *Pali Canon*, such as the *Metta Sutta*, are recited during the *puja*. One of the most popular parts of the *Pali Canon* is the *Dhammapada*, a collection of the Buddha's sayings.

▲ *The palm-leaf books are written in* **Pali**, *an ancient language of India.*

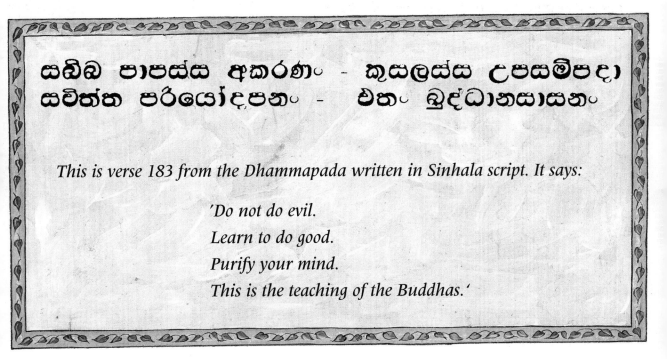

This is verse 183 from the Dhammapada written in Sinhala script. It says:

'Do not do evil.
Learn to do good.
Purify your mind.
This is the teaching of the Buddhas.'

The *Pali Canon* was first written down in Sri Lanka in the 1st century BCE. Before this, the monks remembered it by heart and passed it on by *chanting*.

Buddhist texts are also written in another ancient Indian language, called *Sanskrit*. This is why there are often two spellings for Buddhist words. For example, *Dhamma* is the *Pali* word for the Buddha's teaching. The *Sanskrit* word is *Dharma*.

Time-line

This time-line shows some of the most important dates in the history of Buddhism, particularly *Theravada* Buddhism, and in the founding of the London Buddhist Vihara. The dates are written as BCE (Before the Common Era) and CE (Common Era), a dating system which is shared by members of the different religions.

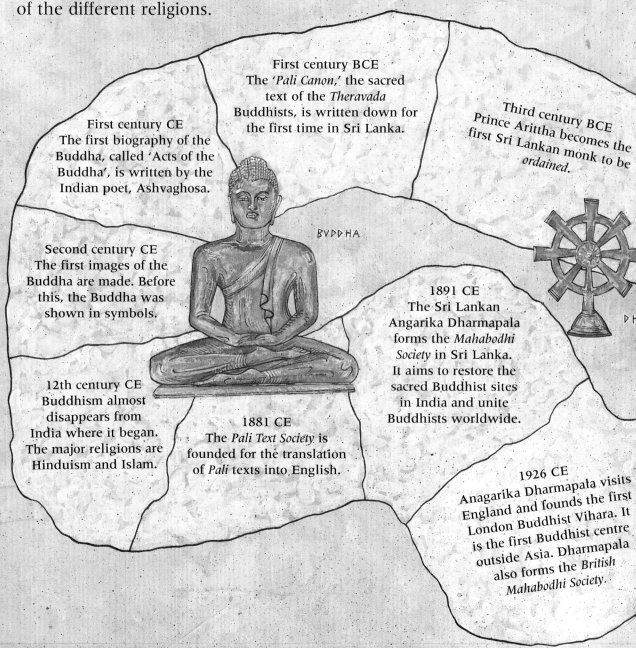

First century BCE
The '*Pali Canon*,' the sacred text of the *Theravada* Buddhists, is written down for the first time in Sri Lanka.

Third century BCE
Prince Aritttha becomes the first Sri Lankan monk to be ordained.

First century CE
The first biography of the Buddha, called 'Acts of the Buddha', is written by the Indian poet, Ashvaghosa.

Second century CE
The first images of the Buddha are made. Before this, the Buddha was shown in symbols.

1891 CE
The Sri Lankan Angarika Dharmapala forms the *Mahabodhi Society* in Sri Lanka. It aims to restore the sacred Buddhist sites in India and unite Buddhists worldwide.

12th century CE
Buddhism almost disappears from India where it began. The major religions are Hinduism and Islam.

1881 CE
The *Pali Text Society* is founded for the translation of *Pali* texts into English.

1926 CE
Anagarika Dharmapala visits England and founds the first London Buddhist Vihara. It is the first Buddhist centre outside Asia. Dharmapala also forms the *British Mahabodhi Society*.

BUDDHA

c. 588 BCE
Siddhartha reaches Bodh Gaya, India where he gains *enlightenment* and becomes the Buddha.

c. 623 BCE
Siddhartha Gautama is born in Lumbini, Nepal. He leaves his father's palace at the age of 29 to search for the meaning of life.

c. 543 BCE
The Buddha passes away in Kushinagara, India, at the age of 80. His followers spread his teachings throughout Asia.

BODHI TREE

c. 543-443 BCE
Two councils are held to collect the Buddha's teachings together. Different schools of thought begin to emerge, including the *Theravada* group. The main *Theravada* countries today are Sri Lanka, Thailand, Burma, Cambodia and Laos.

c. 250 BCE
Buddhism becomes the major faith of India. Emperor Ashoka sends his son and daughter to Sri Lanka to spread the Buddha's teachings. One of the island's first converts is the king of Sri Lanka.

268-239BCE
Reign of Emperor Ashoka in India. He becomes a Buddhist out of the remorse he feels after a bloody battle in which thousands of people are killed.

LONDON BUDDHIST VIHARA

1935 CE
Tenzin Gyatso, the present Dalai Lama, is born in Tibet. Since the Chinese invasion of Tibet in 1959, he has lived in exile in India.

1994 CE
On 21 May, the present London Buddhist Vihara is officially opened. Its new premises were originally built in 1879 and used to be the Bedford Park Club.

1985
The Venerable Dr Medagama Vajiragnana becomes Head of the London Buddhist Vihara.

1988
The Dalai Lama visits London and has an audience with Ven. Dr Vajiragnana.

How to find out more

Visiting the vihara

Everyone is welcome to visit the London Buddhist Vihara at Dharmapala Building, The Avenue, Chiswick, London W4 1UD
Tel: 020 8995 9493 Fax: 020 8994 8130
email: london.vihara@virgin.net

Phone the *vihara* first to book a convenient time to visit. It may be possible for one of the monks to welcome you and talk to you about Buddhism, and show you around the building.

As with any other holy place, you must treat the *vihara* with respect. When you go in, you must leave your shoes, coat and bag in the cloakroom. If you want to take photographs, you must ask first. If you buy any books from the bookstall, put the money in the donations' box. Some books have the price written on them. With others, the amount you pay is up to you.

To find out the location of your nearest *vihara*, look in the places of worship section of your telephone directory, or contact your local SACRE (Standing Advisory Council for Religious Education). For more information and advice, you could also contact The Buddhist Society, 58 Eccleston Square, London SW1V 1PH
Tel: 020 7834 5858 (after 2 p.m.)
Website: www.buddsoc.org.uk

Making a collection of Buddhist artefacts

Putting together a collection of Buddhist artefacts is a good way of learning more about Buddhism. Buddhist centres often have postcards and images of the Buddha for sale.

You could also write to: Tantra Designs, Gas Ferry Road, Bristol BS1 6UN. This is a mail order company selling posters, cards, stickers and images. The following objects will give you a good starter collection:
an image or images of the Buddha - there are various styles from different countries;

incense sticks - for offering to the Buddha;

puja bowls - used to contain offerings;

a prayer wheel (used by Tibetan Buddhists), containing a prayer written on a scroll of paper;

meditation beads.

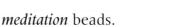

Useful Words

alms Donations of food or clothes given to Buddhist monks.

Bhikkhu A Buddhist monk, one who has given up his possessions and ties with the world to devote his life to the Buddha's teachings.

Bodhisattva An ideal or perfect person who helps to guide others towards *enlightenment*.

Bodhi tree A sacred fig tree under which the Buddha sat when he gained *enlightenment*.

chant To recite a sacred verse by half-singing and half-speaking it.

cremated Buddhists are cremated, or burnt to ashes, when they die.

devotees A word for followers or worshippers.

Dharma (**Dhamma**) The Buddha's teaching. **Dharma** is *Sanskrit*; **Dhamma** is *Pali*.

dukkha Something which is hard to bear, such as pain or unhappiness.

enlightenment Seeing the true meaning of life, as if you are waking up from a dream.

karma and vipaka Your actions, whether good or bad, and the results of those actions, whether good, bad or neutral.

Mahayana One of the two main types of Buddhism. It is mainly practised in Nepal, China, Japan, Tibet, Vietnam and Mongolia.

meditation Concentrating very hard on one thing to clear and focus your mind.

Metta A *Pali* word meaning loving kindness or compassion.

nirvana A state of perfect peace and happiness reached by those who have gained *enlightenment*.

offerings Gifts of flowers, fruit, lights and incense placed in front of the image of the Buddha in the shrine room.

ordained Having become a monk or a nun.

Pali An ancient Indian language. The *Theravada* scriptures were first written down in *Pali*.

pilgrimages Special journeys to a sacred place.

pirith Verses from the sacred texts which are chanted to bring people good luck.

Poya A particularly holy day at the time of the Full Moon each month.

precept A promise or undertaking.

puja The way in which Buddhists pay their respects to the Buddha by chanting sacred verses and making offerings.

relic Part of a holy person's possessions or part of their body, such as their bones or hair.

Sangha The community of Buddhists which includes monks and other *enlightened* people.

Sanskrit An ancient Indian language.

shrine A place of worship, either in a *vihara* or at home.

Sinhala A language spoken in Sri Lanka.

stupa A dome-shaped Buddhist shrine.

Theravada One of the two main types of Buddhism. It is mainly practised in Sri Lanka, Burma, Thailand, Cambodia and Laos.

Vandana A sacred verse which forms part of the Buddhist *puja* ceremony.

vihara A Buddhist monastery or temple where Buddhists can go to worship and where Buddhist monks live.

vinaya The strict set of 227 rules which Buddhist monks follow.

Index

First paperback edition 2000

First published 1998 in hardback by
A & C Black (Publishers) Ltd
35 Bedford Row
London WC1R 4JH

ISBN 0-7136-5498-8

© 1998 A & C Black (Publishers) Ltd

A CIP catalogue record for this book is available from the British Library.

Books in the Keystones series available in hardback:
  Buddhist Vihara
  Hindu Mandir
  Sikh Gurdwara

Acknowledgements

The author and publisher would like to thank Most Ven. Pandith M. Vajiragnana, Richard Jones and all at the London Buddhist Vihara for their help and advice in the preparation of this book. Many thanks to Mr Ronald C. Maddox, General Secretary of the Buddhist Society and his colleagues at the Society. We would also like to thank the staff and children of Southfield Junior School, particularly Alex, Eleanor, Hermeet and Jeffrey.

All photographs by Zul Mukhida except for: pp 3, 9a, 16a, 18, 22 The London Buddhist Vihara; pp 4, 6b, 24a, 25a Ann and Bury Peerless; pp 8, 11b, 19b, 20 (both), 25b TRIP Photo Agency; pp 17b, 24b PANOS Pictures.

All artwork by Vanessa Card.

Printed in Hong Kong
by Wing King Tong Co. Ltd